Copyright © 2023 by Terry Duperon

All rights reserved.

No part of this book may be reproduced in any form or by any electronic or mechanical means, including information storage and retrieval systems, without written permission from the author, except for the use of brief quotations in a book review.

Cover design: Taylor Fris

Hardcover ISBN: 979-8-218-10640-9

Glimpses Of God's Grace
TERRY DUPERON'S PERSONAL TESTIMONY OF GOD'S GRACE

TERRY DUPERON

WITH
CINDY SEITZ

AND
PROFESSOR JOSEPH OFORI-DANKWA

Contents

How It All Began   vii

Chapter 1   1
The Early Days

Chapter 2   6
My Faith Journey

Chapter 3   14
Marrying Leslie

Chapter 4   29
Meeting Sister Laurene

Chapter 5   35
My Father, His Son, My Children

Chapter 6   41
God's Grace and Mercy

Chapter 7   52
Journey to Ghana

Chapter 8   62
My Dreams

Chapter 9   74
Hard-Learned Lessons For Myself

Acknowledgements   83

How It All Begun

I was meeting with Cindy Seitz and Joseph Ofori-Dankwa, having a discussion on how we could get Priscilla Dseagu to the United States.

Priscilla is a very talented young lady from Ghana, Africa, who helps young children with learning disorders. I had the honor of meeting Priscilla when my wife, Leslie, and I traveled to Ghana in January of 2018. Priscilla had attended a class I was teaching regarding following your dream. As one of the class assignments, Priscilla shared her dream of becoming more of a help to the Ghanaian children, and I realized we could actually help her with that. If she were able to come to the United States, we could introduce her to others who had similar dreams.

HOW IT ALL BEGAN

My discussion with Cindy and Joseph turned from a planning session to reflections of our lives. Cindy is my executive assistant at Duperon Corporation and partner with Duperon Education. Joseph is a long-time friend of over twenty-five years who teaches at Saginaw Valley State University.

As I began to share my thoughts, the other two strongly encouraged me to share my testimony. This resulted in numerous interviews and video sessions to capture my words and transcribe them into what you are reading now.

We are constantly surrounded by God's grace and mercy. We often take things for granted; but sometimes God provides us with little glimpses of how He sees things. These take different forms for different people, but for me, there always seems to be an underlying theme: In the midst of my life's most tremendous difficulties, He has never failed to turn them into His best.

Grace is not deserved; it is freely given and I didn't do anything to cause it.

God's grace was always there, but it wasn't until I started working on this book that I was able to see it. It wasn't until I surrendered that I was able to experience it. Once you surrender, you are more open to the grace of God.

Chapter One

THE EARLY DAYS

I grew up on a farm in a little town outside of Saginaw, Michigan, the last of seven children. In my early childhood, we didn't have much, but neither did anybody else that I knew. I never felt poor. It was only after I was much older that I more fully realized how little our family actually had.

MY DREAM TO INVENT

I first became aware that something was wrong with me in the third grade. The teacher had me come up to the front of the class to read a first-grade book, *Dick and Jane*. How humiliating... I couldn't read it. I couldn't do what my classmates could easily do.

TERRY DUPERON

Terry (2) and sister Yvonne (5) on the farm in Indiantown

The teacher asked how I possibly could have gotten to the third grade without knowing how to read a first-grade book.

I didn't know the answer to that question either. She had been my teacher the whole way through. All I knew was that not only did I feel stupid, but the whole school knew I was stupid too. I felt sick to my stomach.

As an adult now, I sometimes wonder how the teacher must have felt. Somehow I had slipped through the cracks. In those days, there was no such thing as dyslexia; at least there was no name for it. Every class just had a dumb kid, and in this case it was me.

Terry (5) at his childhood home in Indiantown

This incident happened at a time when we were studying the great inventors. We talked about inventors like Eli Whitney, Thomas Edison, and Henry Ford. We discussed their inventions, and we talked about how they became famous. These inventors became my heroes, and at the time, I believed that they only had to do *one* thing to then become rich and famous.

Obviously, I discovered later that there is

TERRY DUPERON

much more to it than that; but at the time, in the third grade, that's what I thought. So I became determined that I was going to do that one thing.

I never told my teacher, and I surely didn't tell my parents, about my ambitions. I couldn't take the humiliation or the ridicule which I knew I'd get.

At that young age, my dream of being an inventor and making a living off my inventions influenced everything I did. At home, I began taking apart the farm equipment and then attempting to put it all back together again. Sometimes I actually succeeded; but when I failed, my dad, the hot-headed Frenchman that he was, would holler and jump up and down, totally blowing up when I didn't do it right.

My experimentation wasn't limited to the farm. I took apart all kinds of things. Nothing was safe from me. My sister had a brand new radio and I took that all apart. I never did figure out how to reassemble it. It never worked again. I still regret ruining her radio.

Through all this, I discovered and developed a mechanical aptitude, and I was successful at quite a few of my attempts.

These things, both the successes and the failures, were valuable to me as I grew to adulthood. I've worked several places and tried many things, including inventing stuff. One day, in my early twenties, I opened a piece of mail addressed to me from the government. It said:

United States Patent Office:
Terry Duperon, Inventor

Instantly my third-grade dream came back to my mind. I could hardly believe it: I was an inventor.

Never, ever give up.

I think I have learned more from my failures than from any of my successes. It seems that God is always telling me never to give up.

I need to run with what I've got.

And I must never be the one who limits myself.

Chapter Two

MY FAITH JOURNEY

Growing up, I was raised as a Roman Catholic, but I don't think I ever really knew God. This was confirmed at age seventeen when I found my girlfriend was pregnant with our child. I needed to confide in someone and get some advice, so I went to talk to my priest. He suggested that I might be able to get out of the situation *without* marrying her.

I was truly shocked. This baby was mine — I knew I needed to take responsibility for this. Yet the priest, the representative of the church, was telling me that I could wiggle out of that responsibility? Having grown up on the farm, one of the strong values I had been taught was that, whatever and whenever problems occur, you do not get to run away. You face them and try to solve them. Because of this, I decided I would marry her.

Wedding ceremony at Terry's childhood home, 1961

After that, I found myself questioning everything, and even lost faith in God, because of that priest's advice. In fact, I decided to throw out all of my so-called beliefs — everything, and became a very strong atheist.

TERRY DUPERON

THE FORK IN THE ROAD

From eighteen through twenty-six, I maintained that there was no God. I found that when you are your own Supreme Being, it is pretty hard to be wrong about anything. And so I became an arrogant evangelistic atheist. As my own god, I freely drank, I smoked, and I did everything I was not supposed to do, plus more.

Well, guess what... my life began to fall apart. My dream of being an inventor never totally disappeared, but I stopped doing the things I once loved. Time became a blur. My whole life became a blur. And soon everybody around me could see what I couldn't see: that the life I had built was crumbling down.

I felt a strong sense of doom. I was depressed and felt a terrible desperation. It was like being a zombie: I was alive, but not really living. I had no sense of purpose.

A good friend of mine was a recovering alcoholic, and he invited me to an open Al-Anon meeting for family members and friends of alcoholics. The purpose of my going was ostensibly to help me cope with my wife's addictions that had made our home unstable. Today I might question that, but at any rate, I con-

GLIMPSES OF GOD'S GRACE

tinued to go to Al-Anon meetings, and what happened to me was that my attention eventually was drawn back to myself. Someone posed the question: What was *I* doing to make the home situation better?

Why was this question being directed to me? I had thought of myself as the victim here. At the end of the meeting, a little old lady looked me straight in the eye and instructed me to ask God into my life.

I told her I didn't believe in any of that stuff. She persisted, and softly but firmly said, "Tonight when you are alone, ask God to come into your life — and He will." Funny, I never asked her name, and I never saw her again.

I left the meeting that evening feeling really down and depressed. It felt like dark clouds were closing in over me. In my mind, I could see the little old lady clearly, persuading me. Feeling a near sense of desperation, I knelt down, and even though I didn't think I believed in God, I sincerely asked Him to come into my life.

Nothing happened. It would have helped if there had been a bolt of lightning or something. But there was nothing.

A year or two later, though, something did happen.

Instead of the depression that had been closing in over me, I found that I was full of gratitude, and I didn't know who to be grateful to.

Terry and oldest daughter at Chain Lake in Michigan, 1962

It's hard to describe, but even though life was becoming increasingly harder for me, I began to have an awareness that nothing was defeating me anymore. There could be only one answer: God *had* come into my life.

Yet as life got harder, I got stronger. I felt more competent, more capable of taking care

GLIMPSES OF GOD'S GRACE

of situations, and more emotionally able to deal with it. From that night forward, I realize now that I started to get stronger, and nothing defeated me again. I didn't know it then, but I can see looking back now, this was clearly a glimpse of God's grace.

THE DIVORCE

My marriage was struggling. We had drifted apart and we were both unhappy. We were constantly at each other. I knew, as head of the household, I should do something; but I just didn't have the courage to do it. Besides, God isn't supposed to be telling me to get a divorce. Everybody knows that, even me.

It took some time, but it finally became clear that God was telling me to do something about my family. It was time to make a major move.

I went to my shop that Saturday, and sat in the dark of my office. Nobody was there. Nobody was around. I walked the railroad track outside to clear my mind, and finally came to the conclusion that, on Monday morning, I'd go down to city hall and file for divorce.

We had five children together, and I knew the chances were slim to none that I might get custody of them, but I had to try. No-fault divorce in Michigan was brand new, and I wasn't sure what it was going to look like, but it was clear to me that I had to do it. I wanted to be

November 1971

with the people I loved the most on this earth. I wanted to be involved in the everyday, the good and the bad, and not just a part-time father.

In the end, I first received temporary custody of my children, and eventually gained full custody with no set visitation. Essentially, the children were allowed to be with me at home, and, if the mutual desire was there, they could visit their mother.

Being a single parent was no picnic. I experienced everything. I had never known that moms could do so much, all at the same time. In the past, food was just in the cupboard. Shampoo was just there. I had no idea what it would be like to make sure, week-by-week, that we had milk in the fridge, or to keep the kids clean. I did five loads of wash every single day: two in the morning, and three at night. I loved my children, but at the time I felt like I never got it right. I had no idea how to take care of every single thing.

Somehow I blundered through it. If you were to ask me today if I was a success at parenting, I'd tell you yes.

But then again, my criterion for success was that nobody died, and not one of them did.

Chapter Three

MARRYING LESLIE

After the divorce and going through all the difficulties associated with figuring out how to parent five children alone, I certainly was not interested in dating or going out. However, one day out of the blue, it was clear to me that I should start dating. But I found myself standing in front of a mirror, asking myself, "Who is going to go out with you? You look more like a mother duck." My children were a part of the package, but having five ducklings following me around might not be appealing to a woman.

Regardless, I decided to try, and was surprised that there were women who would go out with me.

And then I met Leslie. It was by accident,

and this is one accident I am very happy about. Maybe it was an accident according to a heavenly plan.

MEETING AND MARRYING LESLIE

She and I traveled in completely different circles. She loved reading and art, and I loved all things mechanical and industrial. I enjoyed designing all kinds of equipment, and she loved history. But I am getting ahead of myself.

How we met was supposed to be a joke — on who, I'm not quite sure. Maybe I'll just let you be the judge of that.

My salesman Bob Premo at B&K Pump was also coaching a softball team the company hosted, and as part of that, he had to notify the players when and where practices were to be held. Bob would normally just call the team members, but this one day he decided to go in person.

Annie, who worked in accounting at Michigan Bean Shippers Association, was on the ball team, so Bob headed over there. Because of how their office was set up, Annie could see who was coming in, and she notified her workmate Leslie. Leslie had some phone experience of dealing with Bob, and knew he was a joker and prankster. So when Annie told Leslie the next person to step inside was going to be Bob Premo, Leslie tried to prepare herself for some harassment. Instead, to her surprise, Bob walked straight into the Bean Shippers supply closet. That gave Leslie the perfect set-up to tease Bob. When he finally came into the office proper, she said to him, "You've got to be Bob Premo!" When asked why she said that, her answer was that only *he* would walk straight into somebody's closet. He was quite surprised, but not for long. Before he took two steps into the reception area, he was ready with his comeback.

"Hey... are you married?" he asked Leslie.

When she said she was not, Bob asked, "Are you looking?"

Leslie, looking at his white head of hair, feared that he was about to ask her out, so she just said a non-committal, "Sorta," but Bob was already reaching for the phone to call me.

"Hey, Terry, I've got a girl here who is just dying to talk to you," and he handed Leslie her phone. Leslie was horrified, yet took the phone. As I chit-chatted with her, thinking I was speaking to Annie, all Leslie could say was, "I am so embarrassed." She said that to everything. Finally, I said, "I bet the other girl at your office is embarrassed too."

GLIMPSES OF GOD'S GRACE

Embarrassed? Why would Annie be embarrassed?

Well, turns out I was talking to "the other girl," so I asked to speak with Annie. I asked the usual things, and then I asked if I could speak with Leslie again.

When Leslie came on the phone, I apologized for Bob's and my own contribution to her embarrassment, and asked if she would at least let me take her to lunch to offset all that. She agreed; and we both fell head-over-heels in love.

She really affected my equilibrium. The first time we went out, we shared a two-hour lunch; and even afterwards, I just couldn't stop thinking about her.

I loved being with her, and still do to this day. It's been over forty years now, and we've even had two children together. It doesn't matter if we're watching TV or driving in the car, I just like being with her.

My previous marriage had been a very unhappy one, full of bickering and backbiting. I sure didn't want to experience that type of marriage again.

Marrying Leslie was one of the best decisions I ever made. It was one of the clearest steps I ever took.

Wedding ceremony at First Baptist Church in Saginaw on November 24, 1979

On the day of the wedding, as she was coming down the aisle on her dad's arm, I had a very clear set of thoughts.

I vowed I would never criticize Leslie for as long as she lives. She had made it twenty-seven

GLIMPSES OF GOD'S GRACE

years without my input. I was sure she could make the rest of her life without any criticism.

It was very difficult at first because I grew up hearing a lot of criticism, and practiced it to an art. But I learned that if you don't criticize, you can't manipulate. If you can't manipulate, you just quit looking for fault.

We all have an idea of what "wife" or "husband" means. And obviously, our ideas are not universal. What if our spouses don't measure up to our ideals? If they fall short, we find fault. But if you release your expectations and avoid criticizing, you quit seeing the faults.

Soon I didn't see any of her faults. I saw the woman God created. I saw the core of her. I was able to see my wife for who she really is. She is a remarkable woman.

Eventually I didn't even see my own faults. I didn't compare myself to anything or anybody. I didn't find fault in anyone. This change in me has been far-reaching. By not criticizing, I am able to see the man or woman that God created.

Let me be clear, though, that when I say I am not critical, it doesn't mean I am passive. I refuse to have people in my life who treat me badly. I am responsible for that.

TERRY DUPERON

Leslie and I had an understanding before we were even married. I told her I wouldn't try to change a hair on her head, but don't try to change one on mine.

I love where my marriage is today. It is comfortable and easy. My wife doesn't look to me for happiness, and I don't look to her for happiness. I just want her to be part of my life. Many people say they are getting married because their spouse-to-be makes them happy. I always ask, "But aren't you happy now?"

I don't owe Leslie anything, and she doesn't owe me. If she doesn't want to make me a meal, I will make my own. If she doesn't want to fold my clothes "just so," I can fold them myself.

The thing about not being critical or manipulative is that you get what is real. If I get a kiss, it is because she wants to give me a kiss.

MY ROLLER COASTER OF FAITH

The ups and downs in my journey of faith surprised me as they happened. My earlier decision to become an atheist had left me joyless and oblivious; and then through Al-Anon, I came to faith again. Good things were finally in my life again; but somehow, I went straight from

TERRY DUPERON

full of faith to zero faith in just a matter of a year or so.

I had just married the love of my life. I knew she was the one for me, and somehow she gracefully became the mother of my kids. Oh, they didn't call her Mom; but she did the things a mom would do. She loved them, and she cooked for them. She cared what happened to them, and she prayed for them, just as any mom would do.

To me, our relationship was a matter of great wonder.

But just a year and a half after the wedding, I suffered a massive heart attack. I was thirty-seven years old, and flatlined twice.

On the way to the hospital, I tossed a cigarette out the window, saying, "Well, that's the last cigarette I'll ever smoke."

I had nobody but myself to blame. I had been a heavy smoker my entire adult life, smoking three packs a day. I had a struggling business, too. I was certain I was going to die that night. What about my business? What would happen to my kids? What about my wife?

In the hospital, I could feel the life go right out of me. The ICU nurse had already given me more morphine than a person could nor-

GLIMPSES OF GOD'S GRACE

mally bear. I found myself praying, asking God to tell me what was going to happen.

In the midst of the pain and my fears, I got a clear understanding of God's answer: *God would be with me whether I lived or whether I died. He wasn't a fortune-teller. He never had been and He never would be.*

With this stunning news, I had a clear and distinct awareness of who God is. I was able to relax, and waited to die. But my journey was not yet over.

LISTENING FOR WHAT'S CLEAR

I spent over two weeks in the hospital, coming close to death several times. It seemed like everything the doctors did was the wrong thing. Every medicine they gave me made me worse. I needed to get out of there.

Finally, after eighteen days, they let me go home. They gave me no medications to take with me, just the instruction to start an exercise program.

This seemed outlandish. In the hospital, I could barely walk from the bed to the door. I had to hang onto the curtain around the bed just to do it. But once at home, I started in on the exercising. At first, I tried to walk out to the

TERRY DUPERON

mailbox and back. When I had mastered that, I would walk out to the first telephone pole. Eventually, I was able to walk twenty minutes out and twenty minutes back, until it got too boring. Then I stepped it up to first walking to one pole and then jogging to the next.

I wasn't back to work yet, so I tried to keep myself busy while recovering. I drove my wife to work, and picked her up again. I painted our front door. I refinished a cabinet.

I worked my way up to running in road races, and finally running the six miles to my office.

During my daily exercise, I would have a little chit-chat with God, but He didn't (or wouldn't) answer my burning question: "Why did you give me a second chance? What am I supposed to *do*?"

But again, God was not playing the fortune-telling game.

One day, I finally got my answer. It was clear as a bell. It felt like He was saying to me, "Terry, will you just pick something? I will help you do it."

Things were going pretty well at home. My children were beginning to adjust to our new family life somewhat, and Leslie and I had our first child together.

24

GLIMPSES OF GOD'S GRACE

But things were going downhill fast at the company.

My stockholders were becoming impatient to make a profit, but it was not forthcoming; even worse, my suppliers were backing away. With no orders coming in, there was no money coming in. I was instructed by the stockholders to close up shop. This was drastic but clear: I needed to do something else.

A curious event occurred right around this time. Leslie had left her career when our daughter was born. Normally, she would be receiving severance pay, but that was not forthcoming either. This bothered her somewhat, but being a busy new mom, she let it ride. She felt that the bookkeeping would eventually catch up.

Suddenly one day, almost a year after she'd left her company, a check for $8,000 came in the mail. It was the answer to our prayer. We started up a new company which we called Duperon Corporation.

With that cash in hand, as well as a big contract for the trash rack I had invented, we were in business. But I vowed that I would never have stockholders or partners again. I would be my own boss, and I would never give up.

On the home front, Leslie and I were lucky

TERRY DUPERON

enough to have another baby, and her life was full and enjoyable, doing what she had always wanted to do. But that didn't mean all of our troubles were over.

The trouble was that, although I was a good inventor, I was a lousy businessman. I kept spending money, but I was falling behind in paying my suppliers... again.

We had done some major jobs, but the national economy was tanking. I had tapped out our creditors again, and nothing we tried was helping. Eventually, we had to lay off most of our employees.

I felt as if I were on a roller coaster: first feeling successful and then feeling like a loser. Where was God when I needed Him? We were winning, we were failing — I almost didn't trust anything anymore, and I sank into a deep depression. I couldn't even get out of bed. I prayed all the time, and also engaged Leslie to join me.

But one day after weeks of this, Leslie told me she loved me desperately and wanted me to get better, but that she could not sink into the depression I was stuck in. She reminded me that there were two little girls downstairs who didn't understand why Daddy was home

GLIMPSES OF GOD'S GRACE

during the daytime — let alone why Daddy was in bed all the time.

She told me that she was willing to pray with me *one time a day,* but that was all. She tried to explain to me that as a mommy, she didn't like to be nagged. She was pretty sure God didn't like nagging either, and that's what we were doing by praying the same thing over and over all day.

And at that, she went downstairs to tend to the children.

This was shocking to me. This was the person who loved me most; this was the person who had the most faith in me... and *this* is what she says to me?

Deep inside, though, I knew she was right. I was in a state of muddle and confusion. I began by telling God I had nothing, not even one idea, to help myself get out of this mess.

But surprisingly, one idea did come to me: *I should do what was clear.*

From that time on, I started to look for what was clear; and it was very clear that I should get out of the bed, and that I needed to take my shower. I should go over to the office and see if there were any messages on the answering machine. If so, I needed to answer

TERRY DUPERON

those calls. If not, I could go home. But I did only that which was clear to do; I did only what was clear at hand. I was beginning to get better.

About this time, my oldest daughter, Tammy, was graduating from college with a business degree. I asked her to come in as a consultant for the company. Turns out, she is a business genius. The first thing she did was to clamp down on my spending. Then, she went about cleaning up our credit, and even managed to get big burly truckers to come hand-deliver money that they owed us.

It was slow going. It was painful. But little by little, we did what was clear to do. Three years later, I did not have even a car payment.

Understand this: I did not mastermind my way out of the depression I'd been in, nor my way out of debt. Even describing it, it sounds strange. But I would start with a clear sharp thought, and then I did it. I never got two steps. I got only one.

But when I took that step, I'd get another. This is how God works. He gives us only one; and to do our part, we must take it. Only then will He give another. To this day, whenever I get a clear thought, I move on it. This is my act of faith.

Chapter Four

MEETING SISTER LAURENE

During this season of my life, I was involved with the Diocese of Saginaw's Serra Club, a club originally established to support the Catholic church and help the bishop. At one meeting that I attended, we had an intriguing speaker: Sister Laurene spoke with a noticeable confidence. She was just a little nun who didn't even own the clothes on her back, yet she exuded peace.

Immediately after the meeting, I sought Sister Laurene out. I asked her how I could have the peace that she had. I needed that sense of tranquility and calmness in my life. Astonishingly, she agreed to meet together, and we had appointments once a week at the monastery for at least a year, but maybe more than that.

Last visit with Sister Laurene in assisted living before her death at age 92

Sister Laurene had been a contemplative nun for forty years, meaning that she spent forty years in silent prayer, and she had just recently come out of the silence.

During those appointments, we had a time of quietness, and then we'd talk. I told her about the severe anxiety I was trying to shed, and the emotional difficulties I was going through. Her input was helpful, but it was really her presence that spoke to me. I saw something in Sister Laurene that was not familiar to me: She was completely free of herself. It felt like Jesus was physically sitting right there with us.

In a setting like that, Jesus would just be with you. He wouldn't be worrying whether He was wearing the right clothes or what He should say. Sister was just like that. She would just be with you, like a conduit of God.

For weeks, we discussed the anxiety I was experiencing, and explored where it came from. I described my business troubles. I explained that, for the first time in my life, I didn't have the next idea. I had nothing.

In talking with her, I revealed that I was fighting depression and anxiety every chance I got. If I let it in, I believed that it would consume me, and I would never be free of it.

She listened to my thoughts, and then she pondered. Apparently, she was waiting to see what God's analysis of the situation was. Only when she had a good handle on it did she answer me.

When she finally spoke, her response shocked me. She said that if I didn't look depression straight in the face — if I didn't let it in — I would never be free of it.

Allow it to come in? Even the thought of it scared me. With astonishment and fear, I went home.

I had gone to her for advice, and I valued it. I could see that her words were straight from God; so when I was all by myself, I tried it.

I went far back into the woods that surrounds our home, and I looked the depression straight in the face. I let it in. I felt it fully; and crying, I felt the whole pain. And I knew the pain already was beginning to leave me.

Thinking about this event, I recall my Aunt Margaret, who was born deaf. What a heartbreak her life might have been. But she lived to the age of 102, and in all that time, never did she develop an illness or chronic condition that most of us get during our later years.

Two of her children had died through the

GLIMPSES OF GOD'S GRACE

years, as did her husband. At each of their funerals, I remember watching Aunt Margaret walk up to her loved one's casket, beating on her chest. She wailed and cried out loud in her grief. She wasn't hushed for the sake of any onlookers. She felt her grief, and fully experienced the pain of her great loss.

Never have I met anyone else in my life who healed faster than Aunt Margaret. I realize now that I was witnessing in real life Sister Laurene's advice: Let it in. Face it. And then anxiety loses its grip.

A more recent lesson Sister Laurene taught me was in a single word: surrender.

After a long hiatus from visiting her, I learned that she had been admitted to a nursing care facility, and I began to visit her again — this time out of sheer love.

She told me on my first visit back, "Terry, when you and I first met, you said you wanted what I had. Now I want what you have. I am lonesome." So every other week, I visited her. Sometimes I came empty-handed; sometimes I brought her a little treat. But always, we would have a nice little chat.

I could see that she was getting more frail as the months wore on. At one of our last visits, as I was telling her my most recent worries and concerns, she did as she always used to: After listening for a long time, she went silent. I almost thought she had fallen asleep. But she hadn't; she was listening to God's voice. And that's when Sister Laurene gave me that one word.

Surrender? To what? To Whom? I guess that was for me to figure out, or to ask God myself. I am still thinking about it. But it means the world to me.

I hope Sister got what she wanted in her final days. She had said she wanted what I had. And that's what I gave her. But it feels like she gave me so much more. It still feels like Sister Laurene was a conduit straight to God. We lost her recently at the age of ninety-two. I feel it deeply. I will never forget her.

It seems like God is slowly taking me by the hand on my faith journey. There are times I have all the faith in the world; and other times where I find I have no faith at all.

Through all these ups and downs, I came up with the method of doing only what is clear at hand.

If it is clear, do it. If it is still muddled, it's just not time yet.

Chapter Five

MY FATHER, HIS SON, MY CHILDREN

MY FATHER AND HIS SON

As I have already mentioned, my dad was a hot-headed Frenchman. Without warning, he would blow up, and I was deeply afraid of him. I actually refused to talk to him because I never knew when he was about to explode. He was wrong, and I was right. He shouldn't be that way, so I simply would not have a conversation with him, even when he tried.

Many years later in a lecture I was attending, the question was posed to the audience: *What price are you willing to pay to be right?*

This made me stop and think; and I went

straight to my relationship with my father. After all, I *was* right — wasn't I? I discovered something about myself that day: I was actually willing to give up the love of my dad. In being right, I had denied my father his son.

Terry's father, Edward Duperon, on his wedding day

It was too late to do anything about it. My father had already died years prior. But I figured I could at least put my newfound discovery on paper. I could still write him a letter, apologizing for my younger self.

I emptied my heart in the letter to my dad (the best I could, being dyslexic). I really wish I could have given it straight to him; but in the end, I re-read it to myself and hoped that he knew my heart, and then I tossed it into the wastebasket.

To this day, I am aware that sometimes I am still too willing to sacrifice the love of someone just to be right. But with that awareness comes the memory of my relationship with Dad. There are some things you never can undo. I hope my dad heard me. I know now that he was doing the best he could. I believe he loved me. And I know I love him.

HIS SON AND MY CHILDREN

When Leslie and I got married, I had one hundred percent custody of my five children. They are Tammy, Terry Jr., Jeffrey, Laura, and Michael. Later on, Leslie and I had two daughters together, Megan and Abbey, for a total of seven children.

I want my children to know me. I am doing the best I can to make sure they do. I really do not want them fearing me the way I feared my dad. In retrospect, I feel like only now am I beginning to understand Dad and his ways.

Left to right: Michael, Abbey, Laura, Megan, Jeffrey, Terry Jr., and Tammy in 1993

Somewhere along the line, I got the clear idea to develop a class to help people identify their dreams. I wanted to help them bring their dreams to life. Being dyslexic, I don't have a large vocabulary, and I don't read a lot of books, so I developed my class primarily from my own life experiences.

I call it *The Class,* and in it we explore our life experiences and brainstorm ideas on how to bring something into the future that does not yet exist. I bring it down to its simplest form.

The Class has had some significant results, both in people's lives and in their businesses. I've had retired lawyers and teachers take *The Class*; high school kids, college graduates, and empty-nesters have participated.

A few years ago, we hosted a reunion where people felt free to take the mic and share what *The Class* meant to them. It was astounding to me to hear what my students said about it, and about me. It was sort of like being at my own wake. They were very kind. Their sharing took hours, and it was all directed at me.

One of my sons and three of my daughters were present, hearing about the wonders of their dad and *The Class*. My offspring heard the whole thing; and two of them turned to Leslie, saying, "I don't think I know my own dad."

My kids all managed to grow up and have families of their own. I know I still have a long way to go in letting them all in, to really know me. But it is still something I hope and pray for.

In fact, I pray for them all the time, and so does Leslie. We pray for them each by name every day, especially through the hard times, that they would have long and happy lives. I feel they are all doing well and I continue to ask God to guide their every step.

A wise counselor convinced me long ago that all you can really do is love your kids. And I do.

Chapter Six

GOD'S GRACE AND MERCY

THE MAN GOD CREATED

Who is this man God created? That is a tough question to answer because I feel I am a moving target. I have no sense of arrival, not in anything I do. I am certain that, even as I am on my deathbed, I will feel like I'm just getting started. To me, it is not acceptable that I don't even try to become the man God created. I am a long way from getting there, but I am aware.

I do believe that this man God created is a man of faith.

For the most part, I am the author of muddle and confusion; but when I get a clear thought, there is more than just me in that

TERRY DUPERON

thought. That one clear thought leads me to take one step, and that one step I take — that's where my faith is. I never ask God for two steps

Cathedral of Mary of the Assumption in Saginaw, where Terry went to school in ninth grade

anymore. That is my trust in Him. I trust God, and I know He will show me another step.

I try to live my entire life in that range: to do only what is clear at hand, to take the step, and to wait. I do not ask God to be a fortune teller.

I do not need to know what the future holds. In fact, it is foolish to even think I could know what will happen next. And I am quite content with that. Those little glimpses influence a major part of my life.

I try not to advise others. I listen to them, and then just share my own experiences, and how those experiences looked to me.

Everybody is on a different journey, and we actually are perfect right where we are. I am not an expert, and am quite certain I don't know what someone else should do. One thing I would suggest is to definitely not follow me. I'm sure there is a better way to do things than how I've done them in the past.

When Leslie and I were first married, she asked me, "Terry, you are my spiritual leader — where are you leading me?"

My reaction was, "Whatever you do, don't follow me. I'm a mess." I really feel inadequate in advising others. I cannot know where God is leading you.

When you look at yourself the way God sees you, you will see someone magnificent right in your mirror. Looking at yourself the way God sees you, you get to see all the good stuff, your strengths, and what makes you a perfect *you*.

Take what you see, take what you know, and run with it. Run with what you've got; it's not about what you're not.

GLIMPSES OF GOD'S GRACE

I get glimpses which come with clarity. I know I have God in my life, and He is my Teacher and Guide. I just know that God is within me and influencing my life. As life goes on, I become more aware of this. It is intangible, except for the fact that I know it.

If I listen, He will show me.

If I head in a direction, He will help me get there.

It may be painful, but God will be with me.

I never pray for wisdom. Wisdom is a paradox. It usually comes from poor judgment.

I'm OK where I am at. I pray every day that I don't get what I deserve. I don't want justice; I want mercy and forgiveness.

GLIMPSES OF GOD'S GRACE

I believe the glimpses of God are those events that have changed my life. I still don't see the whole picture; I just see glimpses. He is so far beyond my capacity that He is not going to give me a bigger look than I can handle. I am on this journey called life, and wherever I am is fine.

In any of my experiences, God has never said, "Shame on you." Instead, it always feels like He takes me by the shoulder and moves me about an inch, telling me He has something more for me. I don't feel He condemns us at all. He will guide us in whatever we are open to.

I ran across a poem by Francis Thompson called *The Hound of Heaven.* It came at a time when I was struggling, and I was delighted to discover that someone else understood me. It's a simple story about a hound that was pursuing a man. The closer the hound came to him, the faster the man ran and the more crookedly he ran, trying to hide as he went. But the hound never let up.

God loves us and pursues us like that, and wants to shower His grace upon us. If you keep running from Him, you'll never receive His grace.

The subject of *The Hound of Heaven* says,

"Lest having Him, I must have naught besides." After reading that line, I knew where I was. I was afraid that if I accepted God, I would have to give up my favorite sins, and I was not willing to do that.

By the end of the poem, the man finds himself in the embrace of the hound.

I finally got it. God would love me no matter what.

It took me a long time to see it. To be accepted by God, I discovered I didn't need to give up anything, or conform to anything, or to shape up. It wasn't about being good. I could simply have God Himself.

But over time, I found I was no longer a prisoner of myself. God took away the need for certain attitudes, habits, and behaviors. Little by little, He has been healing me.

I don't view God as Someone out to get me anymore. Just as in the poem, the closer God got to me, close enough to breathe down my neck, the faster I ran. I now understand that He loves me and cares about what happens to me. I was like the character in *The Hound of Heaven*. He guides me, and I wait for His nudges.

GLIMPSES OF GOD'S GRACE

Today, Terry finally recognizes what the church does.

Throughout my life, I've experienced many glimpses of God's grace. Looking back at these, I see that they have brought me peace. I've stopped with the could've, should've, would'ves. I've stopped depending on what other people think. I love my life, and I have peace. With peace comes acceptance of myself. I'm okay being just the way I am. I don't feel better or less than anyone else, because that is not my concern. I realize that life is about living it, not just observing it.

A good example is a football game. You might be watching a game at home from your couch; or you may be in the stands. You are watching a play, and immediately you are yelling that the quarterback should have thrown the ball this way or that way.

But you are not in the game. You are observing it.

The quarterback, on the other hand, is definitely not observing life on that field. He scans the field, and makes the best play he can make. He is in the field of life.

CHOOSE LIVING. CHOOSE LIFE.

I have never read the entire Bible. I get it in bits and pieces. My favorite story is the Prodigal Son. What it tells me is that you can't do anything good enough to earn and deserve the love of God; nor can you do anything bad enough to lose it. In the story, there are two sons: one good, and one bad. In the father's eyes, however, they couldn't behave in a manner that earned or lost them his love. He just loved them.

One of the most significant things I have read in the Bible is, "When I am afraid, I put my trust in you" (Psalm 56:3). Every morning, I read from the book *Jesus Calling* by Sarah Young, which tells me this. I make myself read it every day for that constant reminder to trust Him (and a little practice in reading).

I believe in grace. I'm not sure exactly what grace looks like, but I think grace is what gives us whatever is just beyond us. It is what we possess that is more than we are. I see those glimpses sometimes, but I'm not so sure I understand it at all.

We don't escape the bad things in life, but I believe that God protects us and gives us what we need. At one time, I couldn't see this at all, and I asked Sister Laurene about it. "Do you really think God intervenes in our lives?"

Her answer was, "You have no idea of the extent of evil in this world." In other words, God is always intervening.

We are so oblivious to this fact, and to what extent we have been spared. If something bad happens to us, we tend to believe it is due to

God's absence. But it is much different than that. I think He even protects us from the evil within ourselves. God is always with us. He helps us cope in tough situations. But we need to remember to listen.

Just because I have a relationship with God doesn't mean He spares me from bad things. He will walk with me through it all, whether good or bad. I am never alone, and I will always have a Teacher and a Guide along my journey.

If we look for God to protect us from every skinned knee, we will be disappointed. God tells us He will always be with us, but He isn't here to protect us from all harm in this world. It isn't much different than what we do with our children.

Our role is to be obedient and to do what is clear. We are to be the hand of Christ on earth. How does this look? How does He use us? It's a ripple effect, the spreading results, that shows the world the hand of God. It is far more than we ourselves are, and so much more far-reaching than we can imagine.

I don't know how to define this more than to simply say it's much greater than we are. We are not smart enough to mastermind it. We sometimes think we can, and we try, but it is simply not possible.

GLIMPSES OF GOD'S GRACE

I heard a story once about gossip. A woman went to confession, and the priest told her, in order to make up for all the gossiping she had done, she should take a feather pillow to the highest hill on a windy day and release all the feathers to the wind, and then go pick them up again. It can't be done, of course. Even though we can still be forgiven, we cannot undo what we've done.

The results of our actions spread like that, and can't be undone. That one action can be for good or for bad.

I think that when the ripple effect of good keeps growing bigger and bigger, we see the hand of God. It is far beyond our own will.

Chapter Seven

JOURNEY TO GHANA

THE INVITATION

Oftentimes in our lives we are not able to see the end results, and we have no idea how far-reaching our actions and our words can be. It is amazing when you experience a very clear thought and are lucky enough to see the end results of the step that you took.

Recently, I was fortunate enough to see that ripple effect in a batch of photos. I was startled into a clear view of having caused something with visible and immediate results. These pictures captured the results that started from one simple event: It was an invitation to visit Ghana, Africa, from my friend Joseph Ofori-Dankwa.

So many people cross our paths every day, every year. Some make little differences in our lives; but some make big differences. I've known Joseph for twenty-five years, and what a difference he has made in my life. He invited me to be a speaker to a college group in his home country of Ghana. I was at a point spiritually where I was looking for clarity, so I acted on it.

But where did it really begin? It started beyond us. There is much more at play than ourselves; we are not the cause of all these results. We simply take the step that makes sense.

MY PERSONAL GHANA EXPERIENCE

On Friday, January 5, 2018, Leslie and I departed from Detroit Metro Airport. We were ready to take the lengthy flight, and to experience the long layovers enroute to Africa. There had been a bad snowstorm in New York which we were lucky enough to miss, and on Saturday, January 6, we arrived at the Ghana Kotoka International Airport. This was Day One of a trip we will never forget.

TERRY DUPERON

Upon our arrival, it was evident that my wife would soon learn how to manage with, literally, only the clothes on her back. We got to Ghana, but her luggage did not. What we thought would be a short delay ended up being a very long delay: The suitcase was finally in our possession the day before we came back home.

Every night, Leslie washed out the clothing she had, and set it to dry on the furniture for wearing again the next day. Sometimes it wasn't quite dry, but I never heard one complaint from her. I already admired my wife; in Ghana that admiration grew.

It seems like there must be a lesson in The Lost Luggage Saga, but in truth, Leslie is just grateful that she took a moment to toss a few extra pieces into her carry-on luggage. I was already out in the car, waiting for her to zip up her suitcase so we could be on our way. Those last items would be what she would wear for the duration of our visit to Ghana.

Leslie was somewhat worried about her wardrobe because she was on the docket to speak to the young collegiates on the topic of "The Empowerment of Women" that week.

One of the other travelers took pity on her,

54

and offered to lend Leslie a brand new blouse to wear onstage. That was such a blessing.

Leslie at the pier at Cape Coast Castle, Ghana, Africa, in January of 2018

And I have to hand it to Joseph — he is the one who pursued the lost luggage. He found out it had been stuck in New York; and once it got to Ghana, Joseph is the one who took Leslie to the airport to retrieve it... just before we were to head back to the United States, but Leslie was just grateful to get it back.

We had such interesting adventures on our

TERRY DUPERON

trip, with visits to historic places, to orphanages, and even to a series of swinging bridges. We were treated like royalty. The facility we stayed in, The Tomreik Hotel in Accra, was exquisite, with gourmet cuisine dining, as well as some American food items; plus we found pure luxury in our rooms. The hotel itself was so very beautiful, the people were very kind, and their service was like no other. The hospitality to which we were treated stands high in our history of travel.

I can say that same thing about everyone we met in Ghana. No matter how rich or poor they were, every single person was gracious and kind.

During my visit to Africa, I met Priscilla Dseagu. After one of my talks, she approached me and we had a brief conversation. That one conversation resulted in so many things, too many to mention here, but the ripple effect of our little chit-chat is still going strong today.

This is an amazing woman I had the pleasure of meeting while in Ghana. Priscilla wants to make a difference in the world in which she lives. Her dream is to work with children with disabilities, and to create opportunities and possibilities for them. She shared her dream

GLIMPSES OF GOD'S GRACE

with me that day, and I wanted to see it happen.

Our conversation resulted in an opportunity for Priscilla to take a trip to the United States. She was able to be here for a month. She worked with several colleagues and centers, and received additional training with children suffering disabilities (including dyslexia and autism), opportunities that she'd never have had in Ghana. Today, she is making a big difference in Ghana, working with children and hosting global conferences where she educates and raises awareness.

The participants of The Class *that Terry taught in Ghana (Priscilla is front row, right.)*

I am also deeply honored and proud to share that Priscilla is opening the Duperon Center of Children with Dyslexia in her homeland. That one conversation has resulted in so much more than I will ever know, but because Priscilla has shared pictures with me, I am able to see just a glimpse.

Another effect of my trip to Africa came from *The Class*, which I had been asked to teach during my trip there.

It created an opportunity and a clear step for Joseph to take. He would continue *The Class*, and teach it himself in Ghana. I can humbly, yet proudly, share that Duperon Education's *The Class* has officially gone global.

It is evident, looking at the photos Priscilla shared, that the one act of invitation by Joseph led us to this point, and it's not over yet. There clearly is more at play here. We simply took the step, and that one step caused it to happen. We are seeing the hand of God in the good of the step.

I had been asked to teach *The Class* over two days at the university in Ghana, and I discussed dream ideas and the skills necessary to accomplish them. Each of my students had dreams for a better future. But the surprise to me was that their dreams were for the benefit of *others*; not one was for personal gain. They were all about how they could serve their communities and their fellow man. They were grateful for their skills and for their strengths, which they might use to make a difference in their own country.

Terry, wearing a scarf that he was presented for speaking, with Joseph Ofori-Dankwa

On January 8, we visited the Canopy Walkway featured at the Kakum National Park. This is a walkway made up of a series of rope-

TERRY DUPERON

style suspension bridges hanging over 130 feet from the ground.

Kakum Canopy Walk in South Ghana

GLIMPSES OF GOD'S GRACE

Even as a young boy, I feared heights. I used to have nightmares about things like that. Still to this day I fear heights, but there, I decided to face my fear, and I walked it. I would do it again today.

Chapter Eight

MY DREAMS

I have big dreams for many things in my life. In particular, I have dreams about God being in my life; my marriage to Leslie; success for my kids, all seven of them; the growth of my business; and the development of my community.

MY DREAM FOR FAITH

For my own life, my biggest dream is to build a faith capacity to fully trust God all the time. The way I do that is by acting and doing, and not having to know the future. He loves me; that is sufficient. I have learned many lessons along the way. Success has nothing to do with what we're not; we just need to run with what we've got. And another lesson is never to be the one who limits me.

These lessons come at a time when we need them most. Most of my problems have come from unrealistic expectations, which I now try to avoid.

This is where I learned not to compare myself to anything or anybody. I try to simply be loyal to the man God created.

I don't do self-help stuff, because that's all about trying to improve. I'm not against improving, but that's not where I go.

If I did, I would have to say that if something's wrong with me, I must fix it. But I don't fix people because, in order to start fixing people, first I'd have to declare them broken.

And I don't know anyone who is broken.

MY DREAM FOR LESLIE

My dream for our marriage is to love Leslie until I die. Over forty years ago when we took our marriage vows, both of us meant every word of them: "To love, and to honor, until death do us part."

Although she doesn't see it herself, I tell her often that if she had not created this refuge, this home, for me to retreat to, I never could have done the things I have done.

Terry and Leslie at Michigan Banner's Heart of the City Award ceremony, 2019

The two of us are like two matched horses, pulling a wagon together. Into the wagon we both placed our hopes and dreams. We pull together. And sometimes it is hard. There have been times when one or the other

GLIMPSES OF GOD'S GRACE

of us has been ill and incapable of doing our part.

In those cases, the other pulls the whole load. If it's hard to pull together, it's even more difficult to pull it alone.

But in all these years, we have never had to toss out any of our hopes or dreams. One of us is capable of pulling the whole wagon alone, but only for a time. It's a job for two.

MY DREAM FOR MY KIDS

My dream for all seven of my children is to leave them in a position that, if I were to die, they won't *need* me. My hope and dream is that they can always provide for their families, and that someday my grandchildren will have the means to raise families of their own.

I recognized very early on that someday I would have to release them, as a mother bird must release her babies to the wind. I would have a delivery date for my children, and by that time, they would have to be able to fend for themselves, and not only survive, but to thrive for having been my children.

As part of this, I had to choose a date to release them; and I decided that since teenagers don't listen to their parents after age sixteen or

TERRY DUPERON

so anyway, I would declare them free American adults at the same time the government does: age eighteen.

Before their nineteenth birthdays, each one needed to find a different place to live. They could go away to college; they could get a place with cousins or friends (or each other); or they could act like the last two, who saw that they weren't going to be spared this eventuality: They saw the writing on the wall, and started squirreling away their birthday and babysitting money, so that by the time their turn came, each had down payments for their own little houses.

Some of the kids left kicking and scratching, and some left voluntarily before their due date. All of them I admired for their tenacity and courage.

Prior to their leaving, I made sure they all knew how to survive out in the wild. They had each learned to cook... mostly so they didn't have to survive on Dad's pork-and-bean special every day of their lives; they each knew how to make appointments, and how to pay bills.

I made sure they all had a clean bill of health, and that anything that needed care had been taken care of.

In 2010 with all the kids

I had also provided jobs for the older kids, which they could have for about a year, until the next one turned sixteen. Being a janitor wasn't anybody's dream job, but it did give them money to buy their first cars and the capacity of finding better jobs more to their liking.

I know it wasn't easy for them to move away from home; I understand that for some, it felt like they were booted, unprepared. But I tried to give them whatever they needed before I launched them on to the rest of their lives.

I hesitate to take any credit or blame for who they are today. I'm sure I had some influence on them, but for good or for bad, I will never know.

In my opinion, all of them are very accomplished in their own endeavors.

MY DREAM FOR MY BUSINESS

I've been instrumental in quite a few businesses as a result of dreaming and of being an inventor. I still enjoy starting new businesses, especially when it helps others realize their dreams.

I started out with B&K Pump Corporation, with a pump of my own design. I had that company for about twelve years, until my stockholders ordered it closed down. I always took great pride in being able to go to a customer's site and design a pump to fit their needs. I didn't have formal training, but what training I needed, somehow I got, and the customers were happy.

Duperon Corporation came next. After being ordered to close the pump company, I wasn't sure what to do next. But that's when Leslie's severance check for $8,000 arrived in the mail from Michigan Bean Shippers Association from her retirement account. Leslie said the reason it came right then was that it was meant to incorporate a new business, and Duperon Corporation was born.

At present, we employ about seventy individuals, representing seventy families who are provided for by my inventions.

The Duperon Corporation team in 2019

I didn't create it as big as it has become. We started out in a spare bedroom, with manufacturing and assembly taking place in the driveway and/or the family garage. Sometimes when I walk through our current space, I am overwhelmed. I still feel like we're a little garage shop; yet I know it wouldn't have existed at all without my presence.

In 1993, my oldest daughter, Tammy, became my business partner, and we have since been joined by another daughter, a granddaughter, and a son-in-law, all earning their positions. I am proud of them, as well as each individual who has come onboard through the years.

I never meant to employ my children because I had seen how badly other companies could treat the boss's kids. But it became abundantly clear that I truly needed Tammy's expertise. Where I was weak, she was strong; and the same for the others. Sometimes we need to put away how we think something should look, and do what is clear.

I still want to continue growing; I still want to provide opportunities for everyone who works at our company. I think it says something that even in difficult years, years of bad economy, and years of COVID-19 and quarantine, Duperon Corporation still bends where it needs to, and it grows, sometimes as much as twenty-five percent a year.

GLIMPSES OF GOD'S GRACE

May of 2019 when Duperon Corporation was awarded Michigan 50 Companies to Watch, Most Engaged Workplace award

Out of Duperon Corporation has come Duperon Education, which has spawned *The Class*. So many have benefited from taking it. I am proud of each and every one of them.

TERRY DUPERON

MY DREAM FOR MY COMMUNITY

Through all this, I have gotten a lot of public attention from the community itself. I have been given community awards for our business efforts. Every time I receive one of these awards, I ask myself on my way to the stage, "How on earth did *I* get *here*?"

And I'm serious. All I see is an old country boy from Indiantown, Michigan, brought up on a farm, and I feel I've never really gotten far from there.

In my thank-you speeches, I just speak from my heart. Other recipients might read a ten-page typed thank-you letter, but I'd never be able to do that.

I'm grateful to my community for the awards they've given me, and especially for their high opinion of me. I really don't feel I've done anything to deserve it, but on receiving the awards, I just say a little bit about myself, and thank them for the honor.

I am not sure how these things happen, but I do feel very honored.

As for my part, I am seeing a shift in myself — a shift to a deep desire to help other people reach their own dreams now. I involve myself with community efforts, such as Mustard Seed

GLIMPSES OF GOD'S GRACE

Shelter, which provides a safe home to single women and women with children experiencing homelessness in Saginaw, Michigan; the local CAN Council's work against child abuse; and the Children's Dyslexia Center's work in the Great Lakes Bay region to bring learning disabled youth up in their reading abilities. After one year of intense specialized work, most of these kids reach and usually even surpass their age-group's reading abilities. I feel fulfilled and proud to help them with this.

Chapter Nine

HARD-LEARNED LESSONS FOR MYSELF

At seventy-nine years of age, and with all I've gone through, there are only three important lessons that I want to share with you. These are quite simply:

1. Have faith in God.
2. Don't let anyone limit you.
3. Never quit.

HAVE FAITH IN GOD

Somewhere around the age of twenty-eight, I had some kind of spiritual awakening. I found that God had not abandoned me, even though I had abandoned Him.

I discovered, after inviting Him into my

GLIMPSES OF GOD'S GRACE

life, that everything was altered. Without the lightning bolt I would have expected, life just began to change.

It took me some time to recognize that fact, but I learned that, even though my life circumstances were getting worse, I was getting stronger. Life got harder for me, but I was able to overcome. And I was able to find a gratitude that had escaped me before. I didn't even know who to be grateful to. But I found myself full of gratitude, even for bad things, because they were teaching me so many things I needed to know.

I realized that I had begun practicing the things of God, without even realizing they were of God.

Think of all the great things in your life. Did you mastermind them? The things and events that meant the most to me were given to me. I didn't cause them. Instead, they were clear at the time, and I opened myself to them. Jesus wants us to know this every day: Stay in the present; trust Him.

I knew that there was Something bigger than I was.

Nothing defeated me ever again.

TERRY DUPERON

Terry (54) doing an installation for Duperon Corporation

DON'T LET ANYONE LIMIT YOU

It was very clear to me: success has nothing to do with what I'm not. I just run with whatever I've got.

Don't be the one who limits yourself. Never say that you're not smart enough, or that you're not good enough.

GLIMPSES OF GOD'S GRACE

You *are* enough.

These two ideas were eye-openers to me, and that's where I started my journey. I really wasn't aware of where it was coming from at the time. It was just clear, and so I believed it, and I did it.

Success or accomplishments in your realm come from simply doing things. You have a dream, and you realize it isn't about what you're not. Once you begin to do that, once you are on a journey where you don't let things limit you, you can achieve things far greater than you can imagine.

I don't get to say who I am, so I quit making judgments based on that. I just try to be that man God created. And I know who that is by recognizing the things I love and care about, things that feed me and make a difference to me.

I love people. I once asked a lot of people what they care about. Young people all said education, jobs, and career; older people said people — their family and friends.

I don't judge myself by comparing myself to anybody else. We do tend to judge people by what we don't have. But I'm not going to compare myself to a person with a full head of hair, while I have none. That's the kind of thing we tend to do with each other.

But, myself, I think I'm at the friends-and-family stage. That is what I love and care most about.

NEVER QUIT

Accomplishments are not recognizable to me because I don't feel I ever arrive. I am still on my journey; and I am always on my way to something else.

With my lack of sense of arrival, it is really difficult to be proud of anything. If I actually arrive someplace, I might say, "Wow, look at what I have done," but I don't feel that way. I never get there. I really don't have a sense of that. There has been so much that really was not of my own doing. All I do is what is clear at hand. All the rest just came.

There is no end to it. The dreams are un-ending. You never come to a point of accom-plishment. Accomplishments are tough. The list of accomplishments in my bio doesn't even sound like me. At one award ceremony, a video was playing in the background. I had no idea who it even was about; and then the speaker introduced *me*. Honestly, I was stunned. That

GLIMPSES OF GOD'S GRACE

was about me? I didn't think I even knew who it was.

The list of accomplishments on that bio all happened in the past. 2005 was the first date listed. I was sixty-two years old. I had an entirely different life before this. I had not really planned anything that was listed in the bio. They just happened when I took a first step, something that was clear to do.

All of life takes place in the present. The more we live in the present, the more we are in a place I call "the realm" — the place where intangible things like imagining, creating, and dreaming exist, flourish, and are rewarded.

During the point in my life that I needed open heart surgery, my priest came to my hospital room just before I went down to the operating room and gave me my last rites. He asked, "Do you believe you have any great thing you need to accomplish before you die?"

My answer was, "No." In God's great scheme of things, I am a really small player. I feel like I'm a speck of sand on the beach. I'm just happy to be on His beach. There is no great accomplishment that I feel I still need to make in the world. I certainly did not set out to have great accomplishments listed behind my name.

TERRY DUPERON

Terry with his patented Flex Link

I don't go into the past, and I don't go into the future. Everything I do is about right *now*. If you do only what is clear at hand, you become completely in the present. And the present is all we really have. But the strangest thing is also true: No matter what we do, it's like a pebble tossed into a lake. It causes a ripple effect, and the ripples affect other people and what they do.

When I started this book, I thought my first glimpse of God's grace was in my late twenties. I now realize that I have always had God's grace.

I believe He gave me grace so it might flow through me. Yet grace is not just for me; it is for a purpose to flow through all of us to others. We are His body on Earth.

Grace is a blessing. It is a gift unearned and undeserved, but it doesn't mean it will be easy.

If you are open and surrender, you too will see God's grace.

Acknowledgements

I would like to express my gratitude to three individuals in my life who have worked with me on this book for the past two years and without whom, frankly, there wouldn't be a book at all.

Reverend Kathy Allbee, the founder and CEO of Released to Reign, had invited me to speak at one of their luncheons. It was there that I shared my story, which was captured on video. Without her invitation, the process of writing would never have begun.

Thanks to Professor Joseph Ofori-Dankwa, my good friend of over twenty years. Joseph has a dream of creating a series of books which will include personal spiritual stories. After sharing the video with Joseph, he thought that my story would be perfect for the first one.

Finally, I want to thank my writing partner, Cindy Seitz. We first met when she began working for Duperon Corporation in 2013.

She is my executive assistant at Duperon Corporation and my business partner in Duperon Education, where we enjoy making a difference in the world around us.